S0-BOI-245

RAISE the FLAG

CLIVE GIFFORD

ILLUSTRATIONS BY TIM BRADFORD

QEB

Quarto is the authority on a wide range of topics.
Quarto educates, entertains and enriches the lives of
our readers—enthusiasts and lovers of hands-on living.
www.quartoknows.com

Author: Clive Gifford
Illustrator: Tim Bradford at IllustrationWeb
Editor: Claudia Martin
Designer: Tracy Killick
Editorial Director: Victoria Garrard
Creative Director: Malena Stojic

© 2018 Quarto Publishing plc

First published in 2018 by QEB Publishing,
an imprint of The Quarto Group.
6 Orchard Road, Suite 100
Lake Forest, CA 92630
T: +1 949 380 7510
F: +1 949 380 7575
www.QuartoKnows.com

All rights reserved. No part of this publication may be
reproduced, stored in a retrieval system, or transmitted
in any form or by any means, electronic, mechanical,
photocopying, recording, or otherwise, without the prior
permission of the publisher, nor be otherwise circulated
in any form of binding or cover other than that in which
it is published and without a similar condition being
imposed on the subsequent purchaser.

A CIP record for this book is available from
the Library of Congress.

ISBN: 978 1 68297 338 7

Manufactured in Shenzhen, China RD052018

9 8 7 6 5 4 3 2 1

MIX
Paper from
responsible sources
FSC® C101537
FSC
www.fsc.org

Picture Credits

Rawpixel.com/Shutterstock 4l; Granger Historical Picture Archive/Alamy 7tl; De Agostini/G Dagli Orti/Getty Images 8l; Chronicle/Alamy 8r; Maurice Joseph/Alamy 11br; Orange Tuesday 12tr; Jeff Dahl 13ctr; Big Cheese Photo LLC/Alamy 17br; Abner Veltier/Shutterstock 19cr; Diego Grandi/Shutterstock 19b; intoit/Shutterstock 21br; Martin Dworschak/Shutterstock 30l; Steve Allen/Shutterstock 32r; Paul Stringer/Shutterstock 34tr; Yulia B/Shutterstock 37cr; S Vincent/Alamy 38cl; Naval Historical Center/US Navy 39t; Railway FX/Shutterstock 40c; Bastianow 41tl; Zippanova 45cl; Ch1902 45cc; Akiramenai 45cr; Ian Dagnall/Alamy 45br; Achim1999 47tl; Kazimirov Vladimir/Shutterstock 51br; Jaan Künnap 52tr; Keystone Pictures USA/Alamy 52b; Henry Bowers 55tl; Granger Historical Picture Archive/Alamy 55tr; National Geographic Creative/Alamy 56bl; NASA Human Space Flight Gallery 57t; NASA/Apollo 11 57br; Ariadna22822/Shutterstock 62l; Getty Images 65br; Anka Agency International/Alamy 67tl; Granger Historical Picture Archive/Alamy 68cr; Denis Dubrovin/Shutterstock 69t; Mark Ralston/AFP/Getty Images 70t; Petr Toman/Shutterstock 71tl; Shadowxfox 75bl; Ecuador Postales/Shutterstock 75cr; Donatas Dabravolskas/Shutterstock 77br; Andrew F Kazmierski/Shutterstock 79cl; Jaume Ollé 80cl; Xinhua/Alamy 80tr; Aris Messinis/AFP/Getty Images 82r; Typonator 85bl; Kyle Lockwood 89br; Neil Burton/Shutterstock 91tl. All additional flag vectors supplied by Shutterstock.

Words in **bold** are explained in the glossary on page 94.

CONTENTS

FLAG-TASTIC

Have you ever seen a flag fluttering and wondered why it looks the way it does and what it's really for? Then you've come to the right place! Flags are pieces of cloth, plastic, or other material that are designed to identify a place or group or to communicate information.

FLAG IT UP!

Flags have broken all sorts of world records! In 2014, at the Punjab Youth Festival in Pakistan, a record-breaking 56,618 people waved flags at the same time (*see above*)! Another record is for the world's most expensive. An American Revolutionary War (1776–1779) battle flag was sold in 2006 for over $12 million.

Every country has its own national flag, while thousands more flags are flown by organizations, cities, or regions.

The design of a national flag can tell you useful things about that country. For example, the 14 stripes in Malaysia's flag are for the country's 14 original states. The Star of David on the flag of Israel is a symbol of many Israelis' Jewish faith.

Many flag designs can be grouped into types. Take a look at the flag types pictured here, then see if you can spot them as you look through the book.

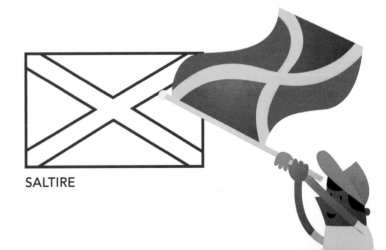

SALTIRE

BORDER

CANTON

CHEVRON

QUARTERLY

SYMMETRIC CROSS

NORDIC CROSS

PALL

FESSES

BORN IN BATTLE

No one knows who made the first flag, but we do know that signs and banners called **standards** were held high by early armies. Over 3,000 years ago, Assyrian and Egyptian soldiers carried signs made of metal or stone. Later, the Chinese and Romans were among the first to carry cloth standards.

Raising a Streamer

Perhaps the very earliest flags were long streamers made of fur or cloth, tied to spears or poles. These were used to show which way the wind was blowing so that arrows could be aimed at the enemy.

FLAG IT UP!

In Central America, from the 14th to 16th centuries, some Aztec warriors carried a flag strapped to their backs called a *pamitl*. It was a pole topped with a "flag" of green feathers plucked from quetzal birds. Some poles were decorated with golden ornaments.

Setting the Standard

As armies grew in size, streamers turned into rectangular battle standards. These were hung from a crossbar fitted to a tall pole and were useful for generals to spot different parts of their armies from afar.

It was an honor to carry a standard into battle, and soldiers would die to protect their standards from capture. In ancient Rome, a standard made of cloth was known as a vexillum.

Giving Up

No one knows who invented the surrender signal of waving a white cloth or flag. We do know that it was already used in China and parts of the Mediterranean 1,800 years ago.

ROMAN ARMY
STANDARD BEARER

KNIGHTS AND HERALDRY

During the Middle Ages, knights were feared on the battlefields of Europe. As knights started to wear helmets over their faces, it was hard to tell them apart. So knights began wearing colors, patterns, and symbols to distinguish them. This developed into a system known as **heraldry**.

FLAG IT UP!

Japanese knights, called **samurai**, had their own system of heraldry. It featured family badges called *mons*. These were displayed on flags, banners, clothing, and armor.

Coats of arms

Some knights flew small pennon flags from their lances and decorated their shields. Others wore decorated clothing known as surcoats. The symbols worn by knights were connected to their family. Over time the symbols developed into **coats of arms**, or shield-shaped designs, that were passed down the generations.

ENGLISH COATS OF ARMS

TENTS AND GRANDSTANDS WERE ERECTED AT TOURNAMENTS, DECORATED WITH BANNERS AND FLAGS.

Heralds

Men called **heralds** were given the task of keeping records of all the different coats of arms. Some heralds traveled with armies so they could identify knights in battle. Common creatures on coats of arms included griffins, fish, unicorns, eagles, and asses (*see left*).

Tournaments

In peacetime, knights competed in tournaments to practice their skills. People flocked to see knights do battle in jousting and other shows of courage. The knights were identified by their surcoats, banners, and pennons—and by dressing their horses in a cloth covering called a caparison.

EVERYONE WANTS A FLAG

As the Middle Ages continued, everyone wanted their own flag! Flags became a way for towns, merchants, and rulers to display their identity—and even to spread their fame to the far corners of the Earth.

Early Advertising

Some of the first flag-flying towns were ports on Europe's Baltic Sea. Hamburg was first, in the 13th century, then Riga, Lübeck, and Bremen. The key on Bremen's flag represented St. Peter, the Christian saint who holds the keys of heaven.

Guilds were groups of merchants or craftspeople who banded together to govern their industry. The flags of guilds often featured symbols to advertise their craft, such as a sheep for the wool guild and an axe for the wood-carvers.

Parts of a Flag

As flag design developed, different parts of flags gained different names:

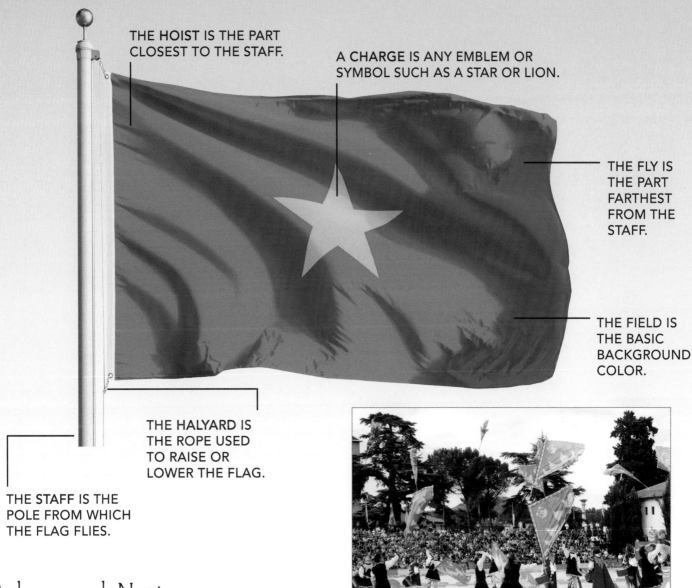

THE **HOIST** IS THE PART CLOSEST TO THE STAFF.

A **CHARGE** IS ANY EMBLEM OR SYMBOL SUCH AS A STAR OR LION.

THE **FLY** IS THE PART FARTHEST FROM THE STAFF.

THE **FIELD** IS THE BASIC BACKGROUND COLOR.

THE **HALYARD** IS THE ROPE USED TO RAISE OR LOWER THE FLAG.

THE **STAFF** IS THE POLE FROM WHICH THE FLAG FLIES.

Rulers and Nations

The earliest national flags were often based on a ruler's coat of arms. When Christopher Columbus sailed across the Atlantic Ocean in 1492, he carried a new flag with the letters F and Y and a cross. The letters represented King Ferdinand and Queen Ysabella of Spain.

Other nations based their flags on their patron saints: In England, the Cross of St. George was adopted in the 13th century.

FLAG IT UP!

In Italy, the sport of flag-throwing began over 650 years ago. Guild flags were never supposed to touch the ground, and competitors, called *sbandieratori*, juggled them to dizzying heights. The sport is still demonstrated at festivals today.

Countries change and so do their flags. Some nations update their design, or a country is taken over by others. In 1991, the breakup of the Soviet Union saw its "Hammer and Sickle" flag no longer in use. What other flags were flown in the past?

FLAG IT UP!

During the Russian Civil War (1917–1921), an independent state was set up in the Chechnya and Dagestan regions, called North Caucasian Emirate. Its flag had stars and a crescent—forming a smiley face!

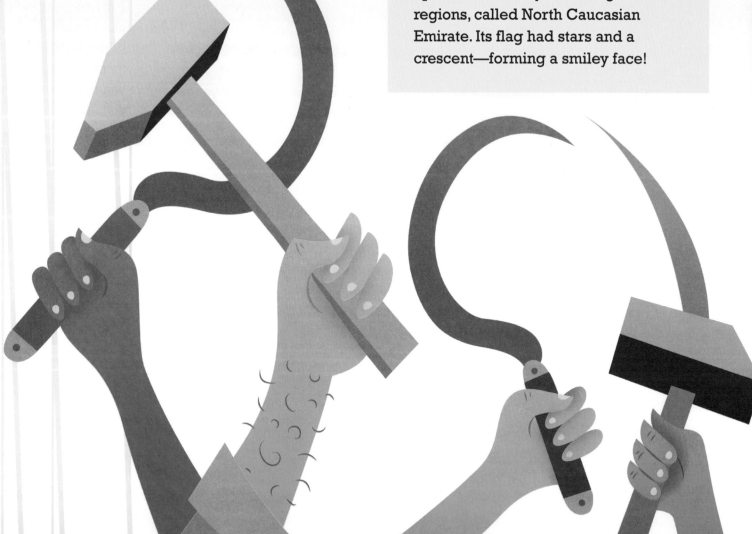

Here Today...

The Soviet Union covered a region now made up of 15 countries. The Union was governed by the principles of communism, in which all workers are valued equally. The hammer on the Soviet flag represented factory workers, while the sickle represented farmers.

The Hammer and Sickle was used from 1923 to 1991, but some former flags lasted even longer. The Most Serene **Republic** of Venice existed for over a thousand years until 1797. Its flag featured a winged lion representing St. Mark. The flag had six trailing tails.

...Gone Tomorrow

Other flags come and go in the blink of an eye. The Republic of Formosa, on the island of Taiwan, lasted just five months in 1895. The republic flew a flag featuring a colorful tiger. The record is held by the South American country Paraguay, which had four flags within a year (1811–1812).

Retired Flags

FLAG OF THE SOVIET UNION 1923–1991

FLAG OF THE REPUBLIC OF FORMOSA 1895

FLAG OF THE REPUBLIC OF VENICE C.1500–1797

FLAG OF ZAIRE (DEMOCRATIC REPUBLIC OF THE CONGO) 1971–1997

NORTH AND CENTRAL AMERICA

There are ten nations that occupy the lands of North and Central America. Each nation has its own distinctive flag, from the intricate flag of Belize to the Stars and Stripes of the United States of America.

BELIZE
*Belize's flag has a mahogany tree, axes, saws, and two woodcutters – all symbols of the forestry industry. Fifty leaves represent 1950, the year the **colony** began its quest for **independence**.*

CANADA

COSTA RICA

EL SALVADOR

GUATEMALA
Two rifles in the flag's center show that Guatemala is prepared to defend itself.

HONDURAS
Blue bands stand for the Caribbean Sea and Pacific Ocean, which the nation lies between.

MEXICO
Green, white, and red were the colors of the Mexican army that won independence from Spain.

NICARAGUA
Nicaragua (along with Dominica) is one of only two nations whose flag contains purple.

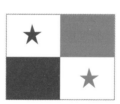

PANAMA

UNITED STATES OF AMERICA

GUATEMALA'S FLAG SHOWS THE COUNTRY'S NATIONAL BIRD, THE RESPLENDENT QUETZAL.

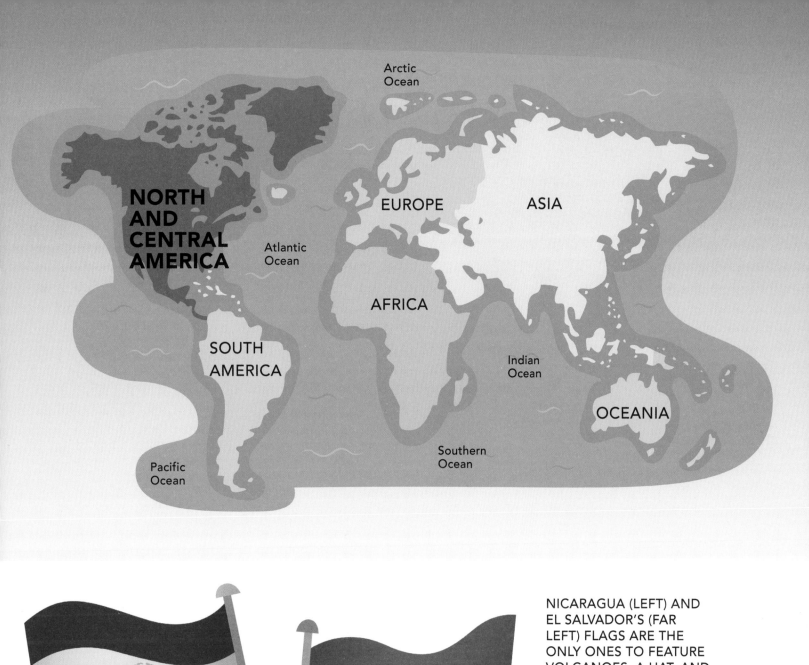

NORTH
AND
CENTRAL
AMERICA

Arctic
Ocean

EUROPE

ASIA

Atlantic
Ocean

AFRICA

SOUTH
AMERICA

Indian
Ocean

OCEANIA

Pacific
Ocean

Southern
Ocean

NICARAGUA (LEFT) AND
EL SALVADOR'S (FAR
LEFT) FLAGS ARE THE
ONLY ONES TO FEATURE
VOLCANOES, A HAT, AND
A RAINBOW! THE HAT IS A
"LIBERTY CAP" AND IS A
SYMBOL OF **REVOLUTION**.

THE STARS AND STRIPES

NORTH AMERICA

United States of America

Atlantic Ocean

Pacific Ocean

SOUTH AMERICA

The United States' flag is one of the world's oldest. A version of it, containing a British Union Jack, was first raised on New Year's Day, 1776, as the colonies fought for independence.

A new version, without the enemy's flag, was approved on June 14, 1777.

More Stripes, More Stars

The flag featured a star and a red or white stripe for each of the 13 colonies. On August 3, 1777, this flag flew for the first time in battle as Fort Stanwix was besieged by British forces.

Inside the fort, soldiers cut up their white shirts and women tore their scarlet petticoats to make the stripes. The blue cloth was the cloak of Captain Abraham Swartwout.

In 1795, two stripes and two stars were added to represent two new states, Kentucky and Vermont. It was this flag design that inspired Francis Scott Key to write *The Star-Spangled Banner*.

In 1818, the stars grew to 20 but the stripes were reduced to 13. Ever since, whenever a new state joined, a star was added to the flag.

IN FORT STANWIX, THE COLONISTS SEW THE STARS AND STRIPES.

THE FLAG OF THE UNITED STATES

FLAG IT UP!

In 1958, the United States was about to add its 49th and 50th states: Alaska and Hawaii. A high school student, Robert G. Heft, created a 50-star design as a project but got only a B- grade! When the design became the nation's new flag, Robert's teacher altered his grade to an A!

FLAGS OF INDEPENDENCE

During the 16th and 17th centuries, settlers from Spain and Britain arrived in Central America, conquering the native peoples. Centuries later, the Central American nations finally won their independence...and flew new flags to represent their proud new countries!

AN EAGLE OVERPOWERS A SNAKE, SHOWING THE MEXICA PEOPLE WHERE TO BUILD THEIR GREAT CITY.

The Eagle Has Landed

According to legend, one day the Mexica people saw an eagle perched on a prickly pear cactus, devouring a snake. They took it as a sign of where to build a new home.

The problem was that the eagle had landed on a tiny island in a swampy lake, Lake Texcoco! Over time, the lake was drained and the city of Tenochtitlan was built in the 14th century. The city eventually grew into modern Mexico City.

Mexico's flag shows the eagle perched above a lake on a cactus, clutching a snake in its beak. The flag was adopted in 1821, shortly after Mexico won independence from Spain.

THE MEXICAN FLAG FLIES IN MEXICO CITY'S CENTRAL SQUARE, CALLED THE ZÓCALO.

Keeping It in the Family

When Panama became a nation in 1903, its leader, Manuel Amador Guerrero, chose a flag drawn by his son. Its blue and red stars and quarters stood for the two Panamanian political parties. White stood for the peace they maintained together.

FLAG IT UP!

Over 8,000 big cargo ships fly the Panama flag, far more than fly the flags of any other country. That is not because Panama has a huge fleet of cargo ships! Companies from other countries register their ships in Panama because taxes are lower there than in most countries.

THE CANADIAN FLAG

Canada
NORTH AMERICA
Atlantic Ocean
Pacific Ocean
SOUTH AMERICA

Canada first started the search for its own flag all the way back in 1925. Flag committees received more than 2,600 designs, but no decision was made on which one to choose for a full 40 years! Take a look at eight of the suggested designs, across the bottom of this page...

A Fresh Start

Canada was using the Red **Ensign** as its flag but it contained a British Union Jack because Canada had been part of the British Empire. As it was now an independent nation, Canada felt it needed a new flag. By the 1960s, a debate was raging over what the new flag should be.

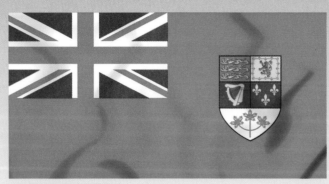

THE RED ENSIGN

THE FLAG OF CANADA

A man called George Stanley suggested a design with a maple leaf in its center. The maple leaf had long been a symbol of Canada. Sap from maple trees had been an important source of sugar for the first Canadian settlers from Europe.

In fact, 1,600 of the flag designs sent to the Canadian government featured maple leaves. Stanley's flag was first flown in 1965.

FLAG IT UP!

The flag on the top of the 300-foot-tall Peace Tower at Canada's Parliament buildings only flies for a day. It is then given away to a member of the public.

You don't have to be a country to have your own flag. Many organizations have produced their own flag, which they fly at their **headquarters** or use during their work.

The Red Cross

In 1863, a committee met in Switzerland to help people wounded in wars. They decided to use a Swiss flag (*see page* 43) to represent their new organization, but with the colors reversed, giving a red cross on white. The organization became known as the Red Cross.

Today, the organization also has two other flags, as the cross is associated with Christianity: the Red Crescent, flown in Muslim countries, because a crescent moon is a symbol of Islam; and the Red Crystal, which is a symbol without links to any religion.

EUROPEAN UNION

AFRICAN UNION

UNITED NATIONS

FLAG IT UP!

People who study flags have their own flag! The flag of the International Federation of **Vexillological** Associations (FIAV) was designed by Klaes Sierksma in 1967. Its knotted ropes represent the friendships of flag experts around the world.

Working Together

Some flags reveal that the organizations they represent bring together people from all nations. The **United Nations** was founded in 1945 to help countries work together for peace. The organization's flag features a world map and olive branches, which are a symbol of peace.

Playing Together

The Olympic flag was designed in 1913 by the founder of the modern Olympics, Baron Pierre de Coubertin. It features five rings, to represent five continents.

SNAP! SNAP AGAIN!

Some national flags look strangely similar. For example, the flags of Chad in Africa and Romania in Europe have the same red, yellow, and blue **tricolor** design—but Romania's blue band is a little lighter. What other lookalikes can be found?

POLAND

MONACO

INDONESIA

Closer than they Seem

Indonesia and Monaco seem to have little in common. One sprawls over more than 13,400 islands in Asia. The other is only three-fifths the size of New York's Central Park. But Indonesia and Monaco share the same design of red and white flag. The only difference is that Indonesia's flag is a little longer.

Turn Monaco or Indonesia's flag upside down and you have the flag of Poland!

Other Way Around

Three African neighbors, Guinea, Senegal, and Mali, share more than **borders**. Their flags are all red, yellow, and green tricolors. Guinea's flag features red nearest the flagpole, while Senegal and Mali's flags start with green. Senegal's flag also contains a green star, which represents hope.

GUINEA

SENEGAL

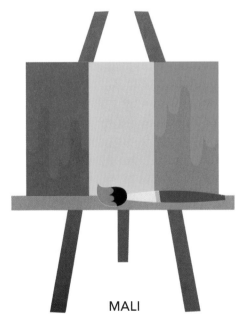

MALI

FLAG IT UP!

Athletes from Haiti (*see page* 72) and Liechtenstein got a shock at the 1936 Olympics. Their national flags were exactly the same! Haiti had first used the design in 1803 when Jean-Jacques Dessalines, a rebel fighting for Haiti's independence from France, tore up the French flag and the red and blue parts were sewn together.

In the year following the Olympics, Liechtenstein added a crown to their flag to avoid confusion (*see above*).

Regions or cities often have their own flags. Some are variations on the national flag, while others are unique. Zheleznogorsk in Russia, where materials for atomic power were made, has a flag showing a bear (representing Russia) wrestling with an atom.

FLAG IT UP!

The Hawaiian flag is the only US state flag containing a flag of a foreign country—a British Union Jack (*see page 43*). The Union Jack is placed on eight stripes to represent Hawaii's eight major islands. The flag was adopted in 1816 by King Kamehameha I, to honor his islands' friendship with Britain.

Symbols of Pride

Many local flags are based on the area's history. Flags of French towns often contain castles or other symbols that date back to the age of heraldry. In Canada, the Nunavut flag shows a traditional **Inuit** land marker, called an *inuksuk*, made of stones. In Norway, the Nordland flag features a centuries-old fishing boat.

LAPLAND, FINLAND

NUNAVUT, CANADA

NORDLAND, NORWAY

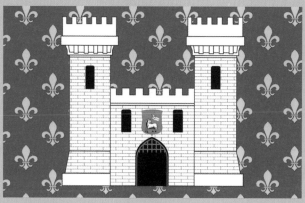

CARCASSONNE, FRANCE

STATE OF
WASHINGTON

STATE OF
LOUISIANA

STATE OF ALABAMA

50 Flags

Each of the 50 US states has its own flag. Some are simple, such as the red diagonal cross of Alabama. Others are more elaborate, such as Louisiana's pelican and chicks. Washington's flag is the only one to feature a US President, George Washington. Oregon's has wagons on the front and a beaver on the back.

ASIA

Home to India and China, the two countries with the world's largest populations, Asia holds more people than any other continent and boasts an incredible collection of national flags. Keep your eyes open for dragons, temples, religious writing, and even carpets!

GREEN REPRESENTS THE RELIGION OF ISLAM, WHILE RED IS FOR COURAGE AND WHITE FOR GENEROSITY. THESE COLORS, PLUS BLACK, ARE ON MANY MIDDLE EASTERN FLAGS.

AFGHANISTAN

Afghanistan has had more than 20 changes of its national flag design.

BAHRAIN

BANGLADESH

BHUTAN

BRUNEI

The upturned hands represent how Brunei gives peace and wealth to its people.

CAMBODIA

CHINA

EAST TIMOR

INDIA

INDONESIA

IRAN

Iran and Iraq's flags feature the Arabic phrase "Allahu Akbar" (God is Great).

IRAQ

ISRAEL

JAPAN

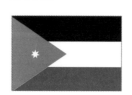

JORDAN

KAZAKHSTAN

KUWAIT

KYRGYZSTAN

LAOS

LEBANON

MALAYSIA

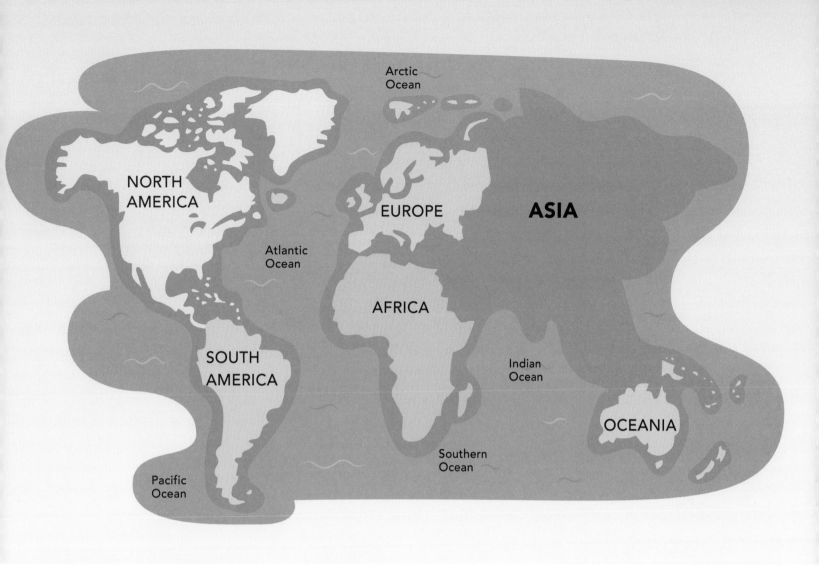

MALDIVES

NORTH KOREA

QATAR

SOUTH KOREA

THAILAND

UZBEKISTAN

MONGOLIA

OMAN

RUSSIA

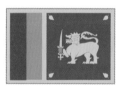

SRI LANKA

TURKEY

The crescent moon represents Islam. The 12 stars are for the 12 months of the Islamic year.

MYANMAR
(BURMA)

PAKISTAN

SAUDI ARABIA

SYRIA

TURKMENISTAN

VIETNAM

NEPAL

PHILIPPINES

SINGAPORE

TAJIKISTAN

UNITED ARAB
EMIRATES

YEMEN

FLYING HIGH

Nations take pride in their flags and the poles they hang them from. Did you know that the four tallest flagpoles are all found in Asia? Quite a competition has been brewing in the continent during the 21st century.

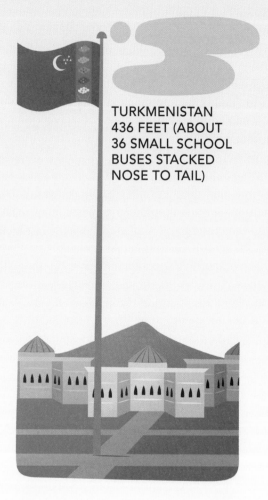

TURKMENISTAN
436 FEET (ABOUT
36 SMALL SCHOOL
BUSES STACKED
NOSE TO TAIL)

FLAG IT UP!

In 2004, the Jordanian city of Aqaba kicked off the competition when it unveiled what was then the world's tallest flagpole, a 426-foot-high whopper! From it hung the flag of Jordan, which has a red triangle containing a seven-pointed star, representing the seven hills on which Amman, Jordan's capital, was founded.

436 feet...

In 2008, a 436-foot flagpole was completed in Turkmenistan. The country's flag features a red band with five patterns used in the country's carpet-making industry. The pattern of olive leaves at the bottom of the band is the same as the one on the United Nations' flag (*see page* 23) and represents peace. The crescent moon represents the religion of Islam.

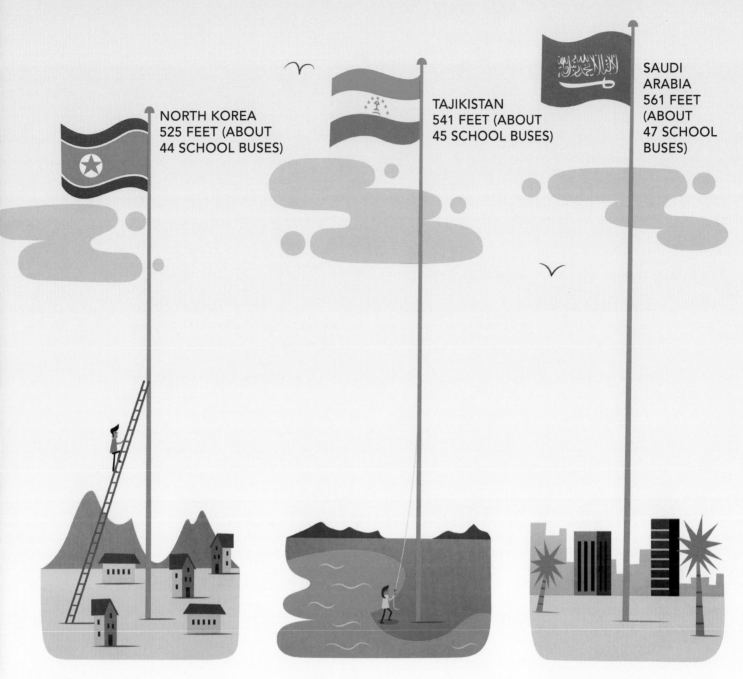

NORTH KOREA
525 FEET (ABOUT
44 SCHOOL BUSES)

TAJIKISTAN
541 FEET (ABOUT
45 SCHOOL BUSES)

SAUDI
ARABIA
561 FEET
(ABOUT
47 SCHOOL
BUSES)

...525 feet...

The North Korean flag
has a red star as a symbol
of their political system,
Communism, in which all
property is shared. The
flag was adopted in 1948
after Korea split into two.
In 2010, North Korea
built a 525-foot flagpole
right on the border with
South Korea.

...541 feet...

Less than a year later,
Tajikistan's 541-foot
Dushanbe flagpole
scooped the world
record. It even has a
weather station at the
top! The country's flag
is a tricolor design with
a central white stripe
that signifies the nation's
cotton industry.

...561 feet!

In 2014, Saudi Arabia
entered the competition
with a 561-foot pole in
the city of Jeddah. It is
three times taller than
Italy's Leaning Tower
of Pisa! The Saudi flag
that flies from it weighs
1,260 pounds—that
is about the weight of
seven men.

THE INDIAN FLAG

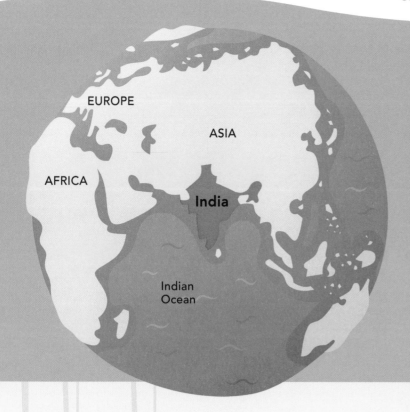

EUROPE

ASIA

AFRICA

India

Indian Ocean

India's flag was born out of the country's struggle for independence from British rule. The great Indian leader Mohandas Gandhi helped to develop the design. But what does the wheel at the center of the design represent?

Spinning Around

Gandhi led India's peaceful fight for independence. Back in 1921, many years before independence was won, Gandhi suggested a striped flag to the artist Pingali Venkayya. At its center was a spinning wheel to show how the Indian people could take control of their own industries from the British. In this case, Gandhi was thinking of the cotton industry.

In 1947, the year India became independent, the national flag was unveiled with an "ashoka chakra" in place of a spinning wheel. This wheel has 24 spokes to represent the 24 hours in a day. It represents the unchanging, never-ending laws of the Universe.

FLAG IT UP!

India's neighbor Nepal boasts the only national flag that does not have four sides. It was originally flown as two separate triangular pennants, which had faces drawn on the sun and moon, before being joined into one five-sided shape by 1962.

THE FLAG OF INDIA

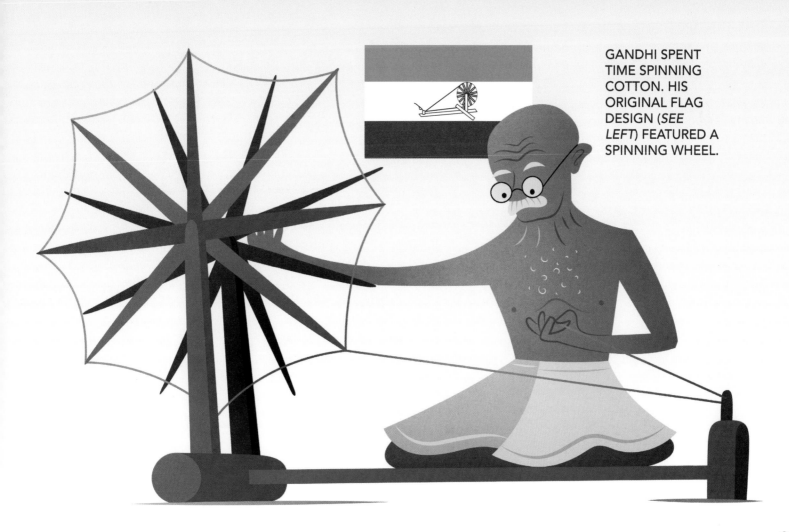
GANDHI SPENT TIME SPINNING COTTON. HIS ORIGINAL FLAG DESIGN (*SEE LEFT*) FEATURED A SPINNING WHEEL.

MOONS, SUNS, AND STARS

Many Asian national flags take their inspiration from the heavens. They feature crescent moons, full moons, suns, and stars. The South Korean flag goes a step further, by representing the Universe itself!

Suns...

Two nations—Bangladesh and Japan—have flags with a red circle, representing the sun. Bangladesh's flag was first used in 1971. Japan's was adopted as the national flag 101 years earlier, but had existed long before. The sun has played a role in Japanese **myths** for centuries, with the emperor thought to be descended from the sun goddess, Amaterasu.

South Korea's central circle contains interlocking red and blue waves. These represent the balancing of the Universe's opposing forces.

FLAG IT UP!

China celebrated placing its own flag on the Moon in 2013 after its *Chang'e-3* spacecraft carrying the *Yutu* or "Jade Rabbit" rover landed on the Moon's surface. The rover beamed back selfies to Earth during its 31-month mission.

...and Stars

The stars on Asian flags often have different meanings. The white star of East Timor's flag is a symbol of hope. The three yellow stars on the Philippines' flag stand for the country's three regions. The four small yellow stars on the Chinese flag represent the different classes of workers in China, all united by the Chinese Communist Party, which is depicted as a big star.

AMATERASU HOLDS THE FLAGS OF (LEFT TO RIGHT) JAPAN, EAST TIMOR, SOUTH KOREA, BANGLADESH, AND THE PHILIPPINES.

TEMPLES AND DRAGONS

Back when it was called the kingdom of Siam, Thailand had an elephant on its flag. This was replaced in 1916 by **symmetrical** stripes after King Vajiravudh spotted an elephant flag displayed upside-down. Some Asian flags still feature amazing animals and architecture.

What's a Wat?

Speaking of elephants, 6,000 of them, along with 300,000 people, were needed to build Cambodia's greatest temple complex at Angkor in the 12th century. The city was the center of the Khmer Empire. Angkor Wat (a wat is a Buddhist temple) is the country's most famous symbol. The building has appeared on different national flag designs since 1860.

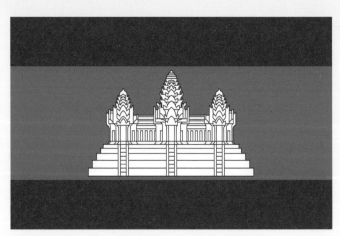

THE FLAG OF CAMBODIA

THE FLAG OF BHUTAN

The Thunder Dragon

One of the most stunning Asian flags is that of the Himalayan mountain kingdom of Bhutan. According to myth, the rumble of storms is the roar of the thunder dragon, Druk. A type of Buddhism, called Drukpa, began when a monastery was founded in the mountains 800 years ago.

Bhutan's first flag, in 1949, featured a small, green dragon. By 1971, when Bhutan joined the United Nations, the dragon was large and white. In each claw is a jewel called a *norbu*, which represents wealth.

FLAG IT UP!

At the center of Kyrgyzstan's flag (*see page* 28) is a design representing a yurt, the tent traditionally used as a home by the nomadic (wandering) people of the country. In fact, the design shows the crisscrossing wood of the yurt's roof. The yurt is surrounded by 40 rays of the sun, which stand for the nation's 40 tribes.

ALL AT SEA

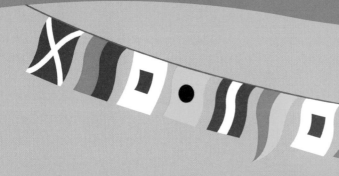

Long before there were radios, flags were handy at sea to let other ships and boats know where you came from or to pass on a message. Even today, flags are used on ships for the same purposes.

FLAG IT UP!

In battles, lowering your ensign meant your ship was surrendering. At the 1797 Battle of Camperdown, the British ship *Venerable* had the top of its mast shot off by the Dutch. A sailor named Jack Crawford climbed what was left of the mast to hammer the flag back up. The British won the battle!

Flying the Flag

Ensigns are large flags that display a ship's nationality. They are flown either from the main mast or from the ship's stern (rear). Jacks are smaller flags flown at the bow (front) of a ship, usually when in a port. Many countries' ensigns and jacks look different from their national flag. For example, the US naval jack used since 2002 features a rattlesnake and the words "Don't tread on me!"

DONT TREAD ON ME

THE UNITED STATES NAVAL JACK

Flags Ahoy!

In 1969, the *International Code of Signals* was published for use by ships worldwide. It has a different flag for each letter or number. These are flown to make important messages, such as:

O = MAN OVERBOARD!

BR = I NEED A HELICOPTER

AC = I AM ABANDONING SHIP

IT = I AM ON FIRE

THE SKULL AND CROSSBONES

Pirates have stolen ships or robbed their contents for thousands of years. A famous age of piracy was the 17th and 18th centuries, when many ships carrying gold and silver were preyed on by ruthless pirates. They used flags to trick and scare their victims.

The Jolly Roger

Pirates would often deceive other ships by displaying a friendly flag as they approached. This is known as "flying **false colors**."

When the pirates got closer, they revealed their identity by raising their own flag. These pirate flags became known as Jolly Rogers, possibly because "Old Roger" was a nickname for the devil. Just one sight of a pirate flag was enough to scare sailors into surrendering.

During the 18th century, several English pirates, including "Black Sam" Bellamy, used a Jolly Roger featuring the "skull and crossbones" we know today. Other fearsome flags included "Calico Jack" Rackham's, which featured crossed swords. Among Rackham's crew were two of the most feared female pirates, Mary Read and Anne Bonney.

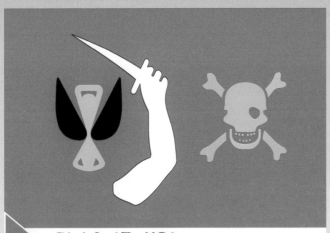

FLAG IT UP!

Most pirate flags were on a black background, but 18th-century British pirate Christopher Moody flew a blood red one. Moody's flag not only featured a skull and crossbones but also an arm with a sword ready to strike, and an hourglass with wings. This was a symbol that time was running out for the crews of other ships!

BARTHOLOMEW ROBERTS

ANNE BONNEY

CALICO JACK RACKHAM

MARY READ

EUROPE

Europe is home to the oldest surviving national flags: Denmark's flag took its current form in around 1370, followed by the Netherlands' flag in 1410. Several new countries emerged in southeastern Europe in the 1990s and 2000s, so Europe is also home to some of the newest national flags.

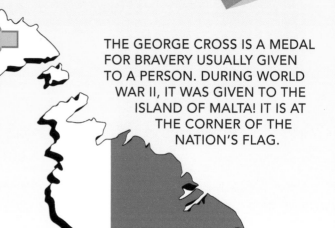

THE GEORGE CROSS IS A MEDAL FOR BRAVERY USUALLY GIVEN TO A PERSON. DURING WORLD WAR II, IT WAS GIVEN TO THE ISLAND OF MALTA! IT IS AT THE CORNER OF THE NATION'S FLAG.

ALBANIA

AZERBAIJAN

BULGARIA

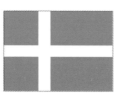

DENMARK

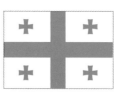

GEORGIA

ICELAND

ANDORRA

BELARUS

CROATIA

ESTONIA

GERMANY

IRELAND

ARMENIA

BELGIUM

CYPRUS

FINLAND

GREECE

ITALY

AUSTRIA

BOSNIA AND HERZEGOVINA

CZECH REPUBLIC

FRANCE

HUNGARY

KOSOVO

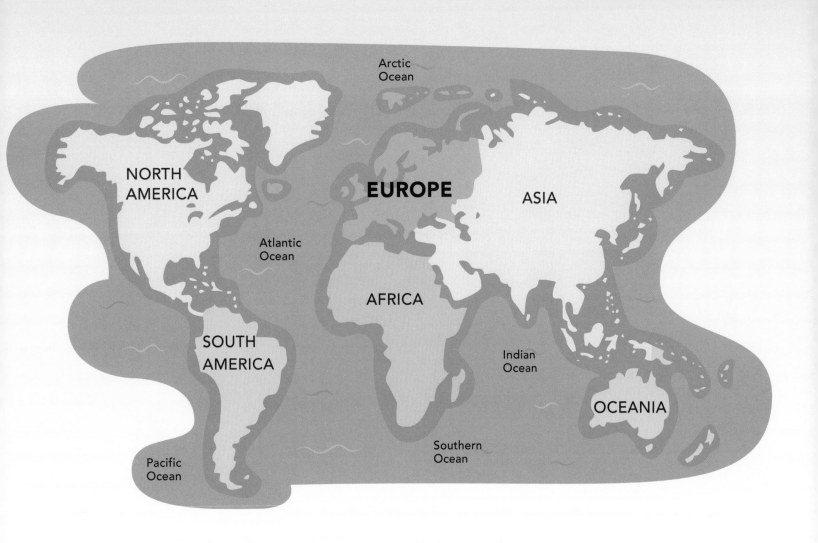

LATVIA

MACEDONIA (FYROM)

MONTENEGRO

PORTUGAL

SLOVAKIA

SWITZERLAND

LIECHTENSTEIN

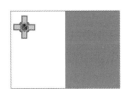

MALTA

NETHERLANDS

ROMANIA

SLOVENIA

UKRAINE

LITHUANIA

MOLDOVA

NORWAY

SAN MARINO

SPAIN

UNITED KINGDOM

LUXEMBOURG

MONACO

POLAND

SERBIA

SWEDEN

VATICAN CITY

THE FRENCH FLAG

NORTH AMERICA

ASIA

EUROPE

France

Atlantic Ocean

AFRICA

Over its history, France's castles and armies have flown many flags, some featuring a lily flower called the fleur-de-lis. Fleurs-de-lis on white was the standard of French kings until the late 18th century. The flag that followed, known as the Tricolor, was copied by country after country!

Flag of Revolution

The first version of the Tricolor ("three colors") flew in 1790: it had vertical bands of red, white, and blue, with red nearest the flagpole.

Red and blue were the colors of Paris, which was at the center of the French Revolution that began in 1789. The revolution overthrew the king in favor of government by the people.

THE FLAG OF FRANCE

KINGDOM
OF FRANCE 1365–1792

FLAG OF GREATER
LEBANON 1920–1943

FLAG OF FRENCH
SUDAN 1880–1960

White, the color of the French king, was sandwiched between red and blue, to show that France's rulers were controlled by the people. In 1794, the colors were reversed, so blue was nearest the flagpole.

Make It Your Own

Countries such as Belgium, Ireland, and Italy based their flags on the Tricolor. Places ruled by France, such as Lebanon and French Sudan, flew a Tricolor with a symbol on the white. For French Sudan, it was a stick man called a *kanaga*.

FLAG IT UP!

In 1830, the French artist Eugène Delacroix painted *Liberty Leading the People*. It shows a woman leading revolutionaries as she waves a French Tricolor. The woman represents "liberty." The painting is said to have inspired the Statue of Liberty, with the flag replaced by a torch.

PRIDE IN THE PAST

Many flags of Europe feature symbols that remember each country's proud past. For example, Belarus's flag (*see page 42*) has a vertical stripe in a pattern traditionally used by the country's weavers.

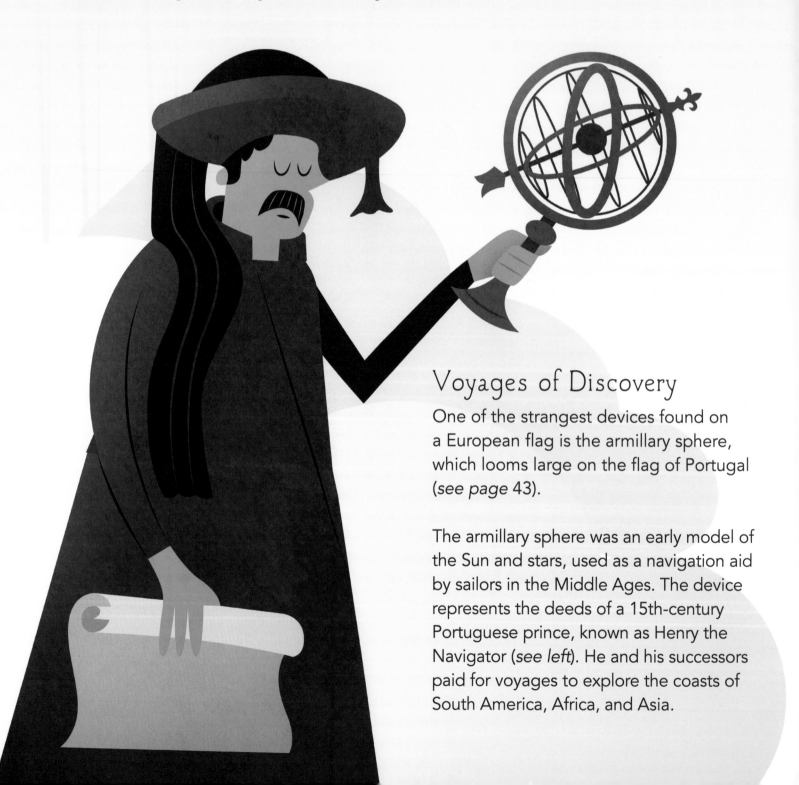

Voyages of Discovery

One of the strangest devices found on a European flag is the armillary sphere, which looms large on the flag of Portugal (*see page 43*).

The armillary sphere was an early model of the Sun and stars, used as a navigation aid by sailors in the Middle Ages. The device represents the deeds of a 15th-century Portuguese prince, known as Henry the Navigator (*see left*). He and his successors paid for voyages to explore the coasts of South America, Africa, and Asia.

FLAG IT UP!

In 1994–1995, Greece and its newly independent neighbor Macedonia had a quarrel over a flag. Macedonia's first flag (*see above*) featured a "Vergina sun"—a 16-pointed star—which the Greeks felt was rightfully theirs. Macedonia agreed to replace it with an 8-rayed sun (*see page* 43).

Freedom or Death!

The Greek flag (*see below*) is known as *I Galanolefki* ("The Blue and White"). The design first flew in 1978 and features the Christian symbol of a cross in the corner.

The flag has nine stripes, which represent the nine **syllables** that make up the Greek phrase meaning "Freedom or Death." The motto was a war cry for the Greeks who fought for independence from Ottoman rule in the 1820s.

Raising the flag is often accompanied by singing the first two verses of the national anthem. The full version is based on a poem called "Hymn to Liberty" and is 158 verses long!

THE UNION JACK

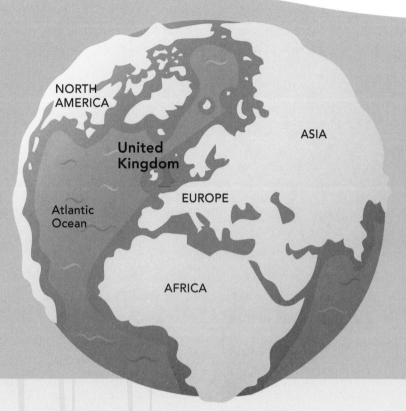

The United Kingdom is made up of four countries: England, Scotland, Wales, and Northern Ireland. Each country has its own flag, but together they fly the Union Flag, often called the "Union Jack." The story of the flag began with the death of the English queen Elizabeth I, in 1603.

Joining Together

For centuries, England flew the cross of St. George, while Scotland flew the St. Andrew's Cross. When Elizabeth I died without having children, her cousin, King James VI of Scotland, also became King James I of England, uniting the countries.

Three years into James's **reign**, a flag was designed that combined the crosses of Scotland and England. Wales, which was already part of the Kingdom of England, was represented by the English cross. When Ireland was added to the union in 1801, a Cross of St. Patrick was added.

FLAG IT UP!

The flag of Wales is called *Y Ddraig Goch* ("The Red Dragon"). A dragon symbol had been used in Wales for over 1,000 years, but the current flag design first flew in 1959. In an ancient Welsh story, called "Lludd and Llefelys," a red dragon fights with an invading white dragon.

THE FLAG OF THE UNITED KINGDOM

Flag of Empire

For a time, the Union Jack flew over more of the world than any other flag. By the early 20th century, the British Empire covered a quarter of the Earth's land!

Today, the Union Jack is still on the flags of independent countries that were once part of the empire, including Australia.

IRELAND'S CROSS OF ST. PATRICK

THE FLAG OF SCOTLAND

THE FLAG OF ENGLAND

NORDIC CROSSES

Sometimes, neighboring nations share similar flag designs. This is the case with the northern European countries Denmark, Finland, Iceland, Norway, and Sweden, known as the Nordic countries (*see pages 42–43*). They share the Nordic cross, also called the Scandinavian cross.

Lopsided Cross

The cross is a symbol of Christianity, but the Nordic cross has the vertical line off-center, nearer the flagpole. The cross was made lopsided in 1748, on the flags of Danish ships, to make the left corners into neat squares.

The design was adopted by the other Nordic nations, using different colors.

Finland's cross is blue to represent its 180,000 lakes. Iceland's cross is red, representing its fiery volcanoes.

THE FLAG OF NORWAY

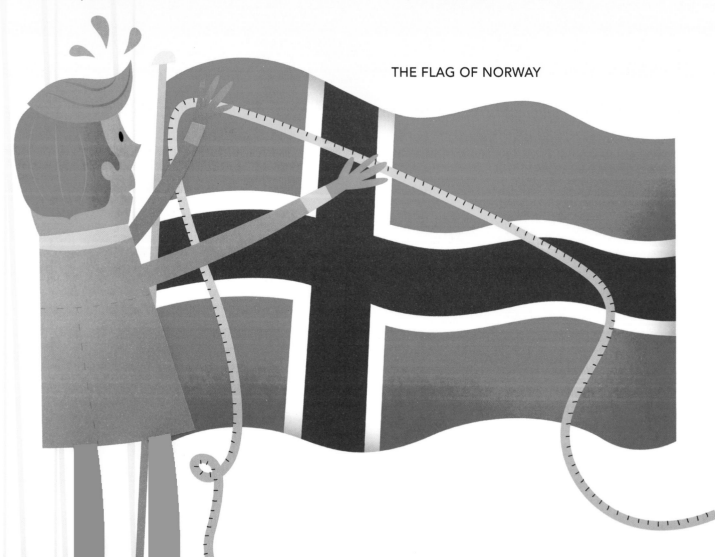

Vikings Abroad

Regions within the Nordic countries also adopted the cross, including the Faroe Islands (part of Denmark) and Åland Islands (part of Finland).

In Scotland, the islands Shetland, Orkney, and Barra also feature a Nordic cross on their flag, to show they were settled by Vikings, who came from Denmark, Norway, and Sweden.

THE FLAG OF THE ÅLAND ISLANDS

THE FLAG OF THE FAROE ISLANDS

FROM LEFT TO RIGHT, THE FLAGS OF ORKNEY, SHETLAND, AND BARRA

FLAG IT UP!

Italy's flag (*see page* 42) has one of the best-known color schemes. There is a story that the famous pizza margherita was first made to honor Princess Margherita of Italy in 1890. The pizza uses the colors of the Italian flag: red tomatoes, white mozzarella cheese, and green basil. This story may not be true, as the dish was eaten long before 1890!

On May 29, 1953, at 11:30 a.m., a Sherpa from Nepal, named Tenzing Norgay, and a New Zealander named Edmund Hillary, became the first to reach the peak of the world's highest mountain, Mount Everest. It was Tenzing's sixth attempt to reach the summit. Now, 29,029 feet above sea level, it was time to fly a flag...or four!

FLAG IT UP!

Since Hillary and Tenzing's ascent of Everest, 4,400 people have reached the top. The first woman to complete the climb was Junko Tabei (*see* above) in 1975. She planted the Japanese flag.

EDMUND HILLARY AND TENZING NORGAY CELEBRATE BEING THE FIRST TO REACH THE SUMMIT OF MOUNT EVEREST.

Flying High

The men could spend only 15 minutes on the summit, as their canisters of oxygen were running low. The air on the peak is too thin to breathe for long. Hillary reached for a camera stored deep inside his clothes to protect it from freezing. Tenzing **unfurled** patches of cloth tied to his ice axe.

The strong winds at the top of the world made the pieces of fabric flutter. They were four small flags: the flag of the United Nations (*see page* 23) as well as the flags of Nepal and India (Tenzing was Nepalese but lived in India) and the United Kingdom (which organized the expedition).

TENZING NORGAY FLIES FOUR FLAGS ON THE SUMMIT OF EVEREST.

FLAGS AT THE POLES

The North and South Poles have proved to be tough places to reach. So, when explorers complete trips to the ends of the Earth, they plant a flag to celebrate their achievement.

WITH HELP FROM HIS SLED-PULLING DOGS, ROALD AMUNDSEN WAS FIRST TO THE SOUTH POLE.

SCOTT'S TEAM ARRIVE SECOND AT THE SOUTH POLE.

(see page 67)

FLAG IT UP!

During a British 1914–1916 expedition to Antarctica, Ernest Shackleton's ship, *Endurance*, was crushed by sea ice (*see above*). The crew escaped, carrying the ship's Royal Standard flag (*see page* 67), and journeyed for months over freezing sea and empty land to safety. In 2002, the flag was sold for £116,000 (over $150,000), a record price for a flag from Europe.

Shivering South Pole

In 1910–1911, there was a race between a British expedition, led by Robert Falcon Scott, and a Norwegian expedition, led by Roald Amundsen, to be first to the South Pole. Trekking through blizzards, the Norwegian team arrived first. On December 14, 1911, all five men of the expedition thrust a bamboo flagpole into the ice.

Thirty-three days later, Scott's team reached the pole and found the Norwegians' flag. Scott and his companions died on the return journey.

Nippy North Pole

Flags planted at the North Pole tend to drift away, as they must be plunged into the floating ice that covers the Arctic Ocean.

To solve the problem, in 2007, the *Mir-1* **submersible** carrying a crew of three dived 13,980 feet to the seabed. Its robotic arm planted a rustproof flagpole carrying the flag of Russia.

THE RUSSIAN FLAG WAS PLANTED IN THE SEABED AT THE NORTH POLE.

FIRST FLAG ON THE MOON

In December 1969, the Apollo 11 Lunar Module landed on the Moon. American astronauts Neil Armstrong and Edwin "Buzz" Aldrin became the first people to set foot on the lunar surface. With them was a very special Stars and Stripes.

Flying without Wind

Because the Moon has little **atmosphere**, there is no breeze to fly a flag. Engineers from the USA's National Aeronautics and Space Administration (NASA) built a flagpole with a crossbar that fitted into a hem sewn along the top of the flag, so the flag would look as if it was fluttering.

In their 21½ hours on the lunar surface, the two astronauts gathered rocks and dust, did experiments, and planted the US flag—an event watched by millions back on Earth.

Sadly, when the astronauts blasted off to return to Earth, the flag was knocked over. Five further Apollo missions also planted US flags on the Moon. They are thought to be still standing.

THE APOLLO 11 MISSION BLASTS OFF.

THE APOLLO 11 CREW, FROM LEFT TO RIGHT: NEIL ARMSTRONG, MICHAEL COLLINS, AND BUZZ ALDRIN

THE FIRST FLAG IS PLANTED ON THE MOON.

FLAG IT UP!

The first flag on the Moon was 5 by 3 feet but was no Space Age design. It was a regular nylon flag bought for just $5.50. While in transit, the flag was wrapped in insulating foil to prevent it from burning up during the heat of touchdown on the Moon.

AFRICA

Many African countries gained independence from European rule in the last 70 years, which is why most of the continent's national flags are modern. Many feature red, green, and black or gold, the "Pan-African" colors— the colors chosen to represent Africa and all its peoples.

ALGERIA

CAMEROON

REPUBLIC OF THE CONGO

ANGOLA

CAPE VERDE

COTE D'IVOIRE

BENIN

CENTRAL AFRICAN REPUBLIC

DJIBOUTI

BOTSWANA

CHAD

EGYPT

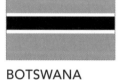
BURKINA FASO

COMOROS

EQUATORIAL GUINEA

BURUNDI

DEMOCRATIC REPUBLIC OF THE CONGO

ERITREA

ETHIOPIA

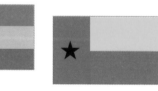
GABON

GAMBIA

GHANA

GUINEA

GUINEA-BISSAU

KENYA

LESOTHO

LIBERIA

LIBYA

MADAGASCAR

MALAWI

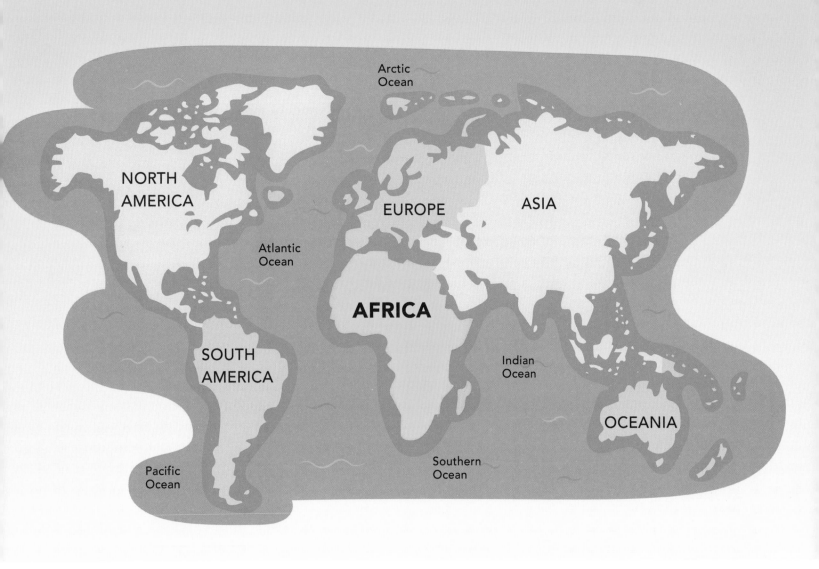

MALI

MOZAMBIQUE

RWANDA

SIERRA LEONE

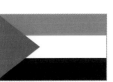

SUDAN

TUNISIA

MAURITANIA

NAMIBIA

SAO TOME
AND PRINCIPE

SOMALIA

SWAZILAND

UGANDA

MAURITIUS

NIGER

SENEGAL

SOUTH AFRICA

TANZANIA

ZAMBIA

MOROCCO

NIGERIA

SEYCHELLES

SOUTH SUDAN

TOGO

ZIMBABWE

STRIPES AND SHIELDS

From 1977 to 2011, Libya could lay claim to the dullest flag in the world—plain green. Many other African nations, however, have flags in a riot of colors and designs, such as the Seychelles' five-striped flag.

FLAG IT UP!

Zimbabwe's flag features a bird based on sculptures found in the ruins of the ancient city of Great Zimbabwe. In 2016, the government made it a crime to sell or use the flag without permission. People who wrap themselves in the flag can spend up to a year in prison!

THE FLAG OF
THE SEYCHELLES

Stars and Stripes

Liberia was founded as a **territory** for freed African-American slaves in 1847. Its flag (*see page 58*), modeled on the US Stars and Stripes, is one of the oldest African flags. It was designed by a committee of seven women and features one star and 11 stripes, which represent 11 of the people who signed the document declaring independence.

Single stars are popular in African flags: the flags of 20 other nations, from Algeria to Zimbabwe, feature a single star.

THE FLAG OF
SWAZILAND

Warriors' Shields

Two nations display traditional warriors' shields on their flags. Kenya's flag first flew in 1963. It features an oval shield, made of the hide of water buffalo and used by the Maasai peoples. With it are two crossed spears, which the Maasai used to hunt, defend their herds, and as a walking stick.

Swaziland's flag features a shield of the Nguni people with feathers called *injobo* at the ends of the handle. This flag was first displayed by Swaziland's King Sobhuza II in 1941 but became the national flag in 1968.

THE FLAG
OF KENYA

AFRICAN FLAG DESIGNERS

African flags have been designed by artists, soldiers, accountants, and students. Togo's flag, for example, was designed by Paul Ahyi in 1960. He went on to become one of Africa's most famous sculptors.

FLAG IT UP!

From 1987 to 2006, Lesotho's flag featured a shield and weapons and was designed by army sergeant Retšelisitsoe Matete. In 2006, a New flag (*see page* 58) was chosen, featuring a traditional straw hat called a *mokorotlo*. The hat's cone shape is said to be based on the shape of Lesotho's Mount Qiloane.

Theodosia Salome Okoh

Ghana's flag was the work of a schoolteacher, Theodosia Salome Okoh (*see above*). She chose green to represent Ghana's plants, yellow for its gold, and red for the blood of those who died fighting for independence.

Okoh also **pioneered** the sport of hockey in Ghana. When she died in 2015, aged 92, all flags in the country were flown at **half-mast** for three days.

Taiwo Akinkunmi

Nigeria's flag (*see page 59*) was designed by a 23-year-old Nigerian-born student in London. Taiwo Akinkunmi heard about a competition to design the flag in 1958. He mailed off his green and white design, which contained a sun in the middle (*see below*), and thought little of it until he received a $130 prize—even though the design used no longer included the sun. Akinkunmi returned to Nigeria and lives in a house painted green and white!

FLAG OF FREEDOM

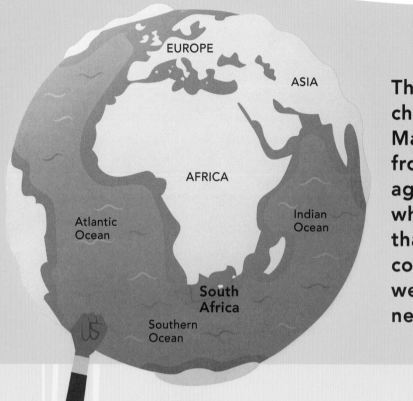

EUROPE

ASIA

AFRICA

Atlantic
Ocean

Indian
Ocean

South
Africa

Southern
Ocean

The early 1990s were a time of change in South Africa. Nelson Mandela had just been released from prison. He had led the fight against the apartheid system, which gave fewer rights to black than white South Africans. The country's first free elections were to be held in 1994, and a new flag was needed...fast!

A Flag in a Week

First of all, South Africa held a competition for a new flag. There were 7,000 entries, but no design seemed right. In late 1993, designer Frederick Brownell was given just a week to come up with an amazing new flag.

NELSON MANDELA WAS ELECTED THE FIRST BLACK PRESIDENT OF SOUTH AFRICA IN 1994.

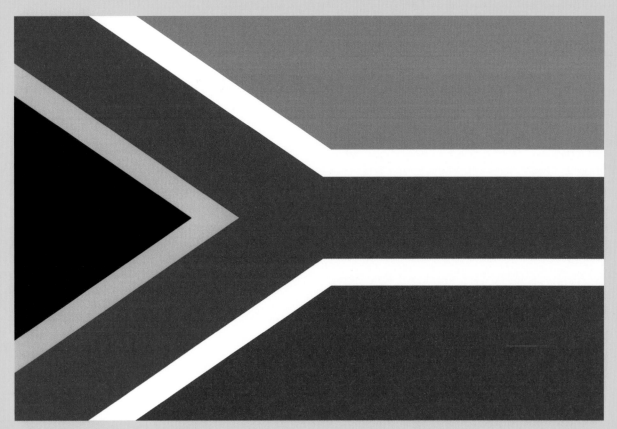

THE FLAG OF SOUTH AFRICA

Luckily, Brownell had already made sketches for a flag while bored during a conference in Switzerland! He chose a Y shape representing different South African peoples uniting as one. When Brownell's design was sent to Nelson Mandela for approval, it came out of the **fax machine** in black and white. Someone dashed to the store to buy pencils to color it in!

Just in Time!

Now there was a rush to produce 100,000 flags in time! The flag makers in Europe ran out of material and had to fly in more from Japan. Finally, the flag was draped over the parliament buildings when Mandela came to power in May 1994.

FLAG IT UP!

The South African flag is the only African flag that has flown both at the top of Mount Everest (in 1996) and in space (in 2002), when Africa's first astronaut, Mark Shuttleworth, traveled on board the *Soyuz* spacecraft and the *International Space Station*.

COMMUNICATING WITH FLAGS

Flags are often used to give people useful—or even life-saving—information. Some methods of signaling with flags use the color or pattern of flags to give information. But let's start by looking at how the position of flags can be used to send messages.

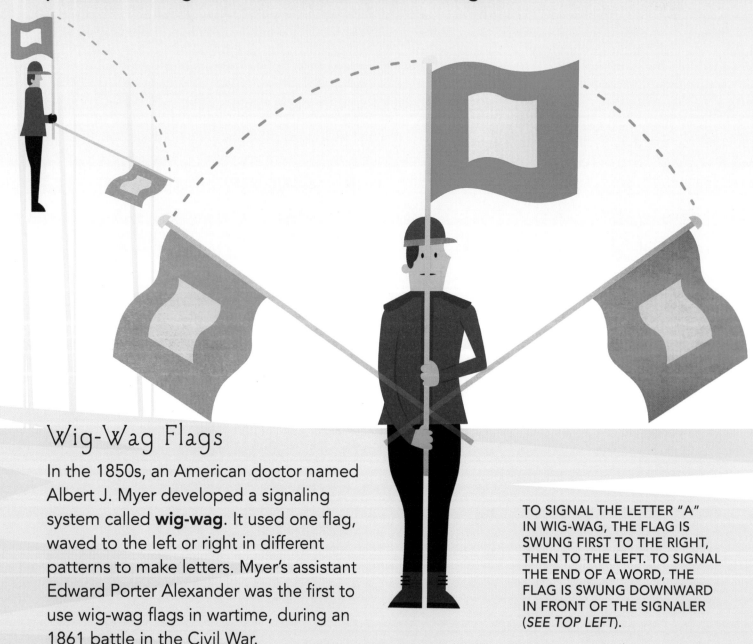

Wig-Wag Flags

In the 1850s, an American doctor named Albert J. Myer developed a signaling system called **wig-wag**. It used one flag, waved to the left or right in different patterns to make letters. Myer's assistant Edward Porter Alexander was the first to use wig-wag flags in wartime, during an 1861 battle in the Civil War.

TO SIGNAL THE LETTER "A" IN WIG-WAG, THE FLAG IS SWUNG FIRST TO THE RIGHT, THEN TO THE LEFT. TO SIGNAL THE END OF A WORD, THE FLAG IS SWUNG DOWNWARD IN FRONT OF THE SIGNALER (*SEE TOP LEFT*).

FLAG IT UP!

Many countries use red flags on beaches to signal dangerous swimming areas. In Australia and other countries, a red and yellow flag shows that the beach is patrolled by lifeguards. On some South African beaches, a shark flag is flown when a shark is circling…

I'm at Home

In the UK, raising the Royal Standard flag above a palace reveals that Queen Elizabeth II is staying. It is also raised on a car or ship when the Queen is on it.

The flag has four quarters, two representing England and one each for Scotland and Ireland. Wales is not featured, as it is represented on the standard of the Prince of Wales, the oldest son of the king or queen.

A ROYAL STANDARD FLIES OVER WINDSOR CASTLE.

SEMAPHORE

In the 1790s, France was at war, having just overthrown its king. The Chappe brothers built a series of towers to send messages across France in hours. This was many times faster than messengers on horseback in a time long before the radio or telephone. The system became known as semaphore.

BLUE AND WHITE SEMAPHORE FLAGS ARE USED ON LAND.

▶ FLAG IT UP!

During World War II (1939–1945), US ships were firing on Japanese forces in the Philippines (*see above*). Three Filipino men who had been Boy Scouts, Valeriano Abello, Antero Junia, and Vicente Tistón, signaled to the US ships using diapers as semaphore flags. They directed the ships to fire only on the Japanese positions, stopping them from accidentally killing Filipino civilians.

Pass It On

Claude Chappe and his brothers built 530 towers, 6–10 miles apart. The towers had arms that could be set in different positions to represent letters. People at one tower would view the previous tower's signals then set the arms on their tower to match, passing on the signal.

Out at Sea

Navies started using the semaphore system in the early 1800s, but instead of towers, they used a sailor holding two flags. Semaphore flags were often used by the armed forces during World War I (1914–1918). Many Boy and Girl Scouts also learned how to signal.

The flags have developed into square designs split diagonally into two colors. Red and yellow flags are used at sea, while blue and white are used on land.

Semaphore Signals

REST/SPACE A – 1 B – 2 C – 3 D – 4 E – 5

F – 6 G – 7 H – 8 I – 9 J – 0 K

L M N O P Q

R S T U V W

X Y Z NUMERALS ERROR/ATTENTION CANCEL

O   ANY WORD OR NUMBER CAN BE SPELLED OUT USING TWO FLAGS.   K

SPORTS FLAGS

FRENCH PARALYMPIAN LONG JUMPER XAVIER LE DRAOULLEC IS GIVEN A RED FLAG FOR A FOUL JUMP.

Flags are used in many sports— and not just by the fans who wave them in the stands. In sports such as soccer, flags mark the corners of the pitch, while in golf they mark the positions of the holes.

It's Good, It's Bad...

Officials in athletics use flags to signal if a throw or jump is valid. In the long jump, a red flag signals a foul jump and a white flag is shown when a jump is good.

Flags are also used to show that a goal or point has been scored, such as a green flag in Gaelic football. In soccer, referee's assistants use a single flag to communicate which team gets to take a throw-in or when the game will be restarted with a corner or goal kick.

FLAG IT UP!

American football officials carry yellow penalty flags which they throw onto the field if they spot a player breaking the rules. These flags used to be weighted with steel ball bearings, until 1999, when a flag hit Cleveland Browns player Orlando Brown in the eye and stopped him from playing until 2003.

F1 Flags

FLAG MARSHALS AT GRAND PRIX RACES USE FLAGS TO COMMUNICATE WITH DRIVERS AS THEY WHIZ BY.

Warns that the race has been stopped for safety reasons.

Signals that a problem on the track has been cleared away.

Shown to one driver to signal that a car is trying to overtake.

Warns all cars that the track is slippery.

Warns a driver that their car has a problem and should leave the track.

Warns a driver for doing something wrong.

Racing through the Dust

A black and white checkered flag is waved at the end of most motor races. Early motor racing was often on dirt tracks and the flag's pattern could still be seen by drivers and fans through the dust thrown up by the cars' wheels.

SOUTH AMERICA AND THE CARIBBEAN

The continent of South America has 12 independent countries. Most of the islands that make up the 13 independent nations in the Caribbean Sea were once colonies of countries such as France or Britain. Look closely to see how some of these flags reveal their country's history.

SISSEROU PARROT

ANTIGUA AND BARBUDA

BOLIVIA

COLOMBIA

DOMINICAN REPUBLIC

HAITI

ST. KITTS AND NEVIS

ARGENTINA

BRAZIL

CUBA

ECUADOR

JAMAICA

ST. LUCIA

BAHAMAS

CHILE

Blue stands for sea, red for the Chilean people, and white for the snow-capped mountains.

DOMINICA

Dominica's flag features a very rare bird, the sisserou parrot. Fewer than 400 of them survive.

GRENADA

PARAGUAY

ST. VINCENT AND THE GRENADINES

BARBADOS

GUYANA

PERU

SURINAME

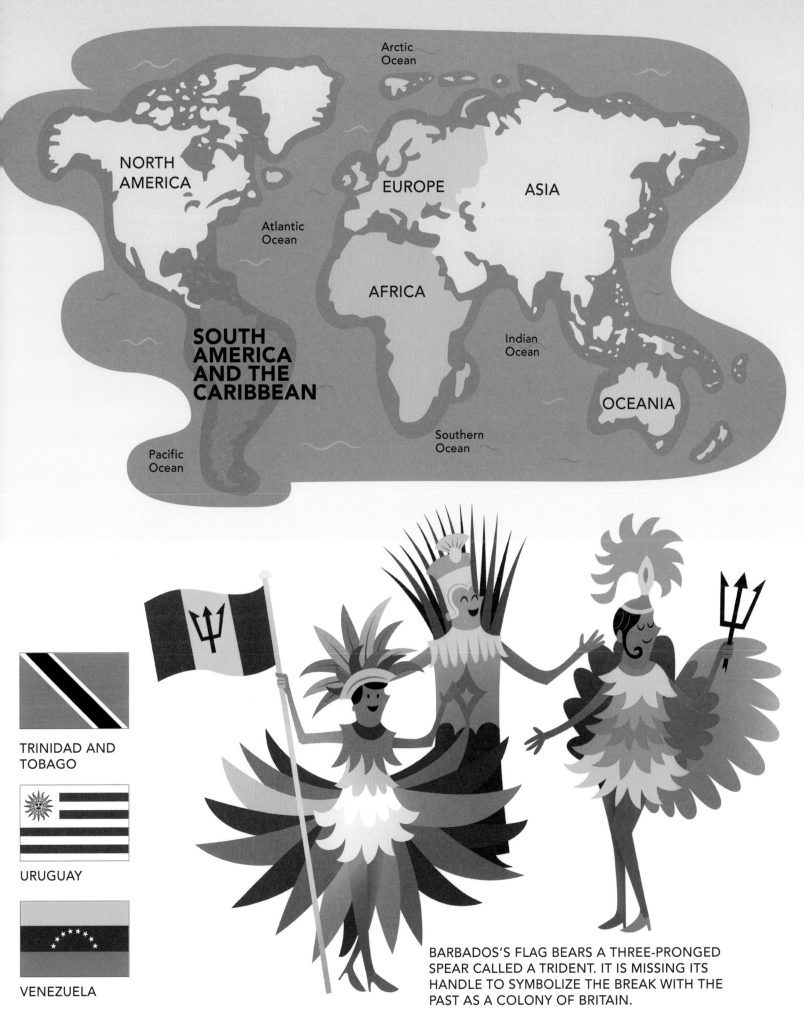

NORTH
AMERICA

Arctic
Ocean

EUROPE

ASIA

Atlantic
Ocean

AFRICA

SOUTH
AMERICA
AND THE
CARIBBEAN

Indian
Ocean

OCEANIA

Pacific
Ocean

Southern
Ocean

TRINIDAD AND
TOBAGO

URUGUAY

VENEZUELA

BARBADOS'S FLAG BEARS A THREE-PRONGED
SPEAR CALLED A TRIDENT. IT IS MISSING ITS
HANDLE TO SYMBOLIZE THE BREAK WITH THE
PAST AS A COLONY OF BRITAIN.

FLAGS IN COMMON

Some South American and Caribbean flags look strangely similar. Look at the Cuban and Puerto Rican flags below... Both flags were designed in the 19th century by islanders living in **exile** in New York City while fighting for the islands' independence from Spain.

THE GOLDEN SUNS OF ARGENTINA (LEFT) AND URUGUAY (RIGHT)

THE FLAG OF CUBA, A COUNTRY IN THE CARIBBEAN

THE FLAG OF PUERTO RICO, A US TERRITORY

AN ANDEAN CONDOR

Copy Cats

Argentina began its struggle against Spanish rule in 1810. In 1812, one of its rebel leaders, Manuel Belgrano, came up with a new flag to fight under, using light blue and white. In 1818, a sun was added to the flag (*see page 72*). In Uruguay, politician Joaquín Suárez was inspired by Argentina's flag when he created a design for Uruguay in 1828. It featured light blue and white stripes and a sun (*see page 73*)!

Sticking Together

Around the same time, a chunk of South America formed a nation known as Gran Colombia. Its flag had red, blue, and yellow stripes. After Gran Colombia broke up in 1830, three of its territories, Venezuela, Colombia, and Ecuador, adopted similar designs for the flags of their new countries (*see pages 72–73*).

FLAG IT UP!

Ecuador's flag (*see page 72*) features the country's tallest volcano, Mount Chimborazo (*see above*); the Guayas River; South America's first oceangoing steamboat, the *Guayas*, built in 1841; and an Andean condor.

Ecuador's is the only national flag to feature four signs of the zodiac: Aries (a goat), Taurus (a bull), Gemini (twins), and Cancer (a crab). These represent the months March to July 1845, when a revolution took place.

FLAG OF GRAN COLOMBIA 1822–1830

SAY IT WITH COLOR

Jamaica's flag is the only national flag that does not contain any of the colors red, white, and blue. Instead, Jamaica chose black to represent the strength of its people, yellow for its wealth and golden sunshine, and green for its lush plants.

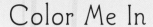

JAMAICA

Color Me In

The flag of Guyana, nicknamed "The Golden Arrowhead," became the national flag after the South American country gained independence from Britain in 1966. The flag was designed by American Whitney Smith and the first flag was sewn by his mom! Smith went on to become a flag expert and even created the term "vexillology" to describe the study of flags.

The green on the flag represents farming, white is for rivers, gold is for mineral wealth, black is for strength, and red is for energy.

MRS. SMITH SEWS THE FIRST GUYANESE FLAG.

THE BACK OF PARAGUAY'S FLAG

THE FRONT OF PARAGUAY'S FLAG

Lion-Hearted

Paraguay based its flag on the colors of the French Tricolor (*see pages 44–45*), which came to represent freedom during the French Revolution.

Paraguay's is the only national flag in the world today to have a different design on the front and back (*see above*). On the front is the country's coat of arms, while on the back is a circular seal with a lion and the words "Peace and justice" in Spanish.

FLAG IT UP!

Brazil's green and yellow flag features a globe containing 27 stars. It was designed by mathematician Raimundo Teixeira Mendes. It shows the night sky above the capital city, Rio de Janeiro, on November 15, 1889, when Brazil became a republic. Each star represents one of Brazil's 27 states.

FLYING THE FLAG

Most countries have detailed rules about the size and colors of their national flags and how the flag should be treated. Some nations do not allow their flag to appear in advertising, while most countries require their flags to be raised at sunrise and lowered at sunset.

Flag Etiquette

Ways of folding and flying a flag are called flag etiquette. A common piece of flag etiquette is that flags are lowered part way down the flagpole as a sign of mourning after the death of a leader or a disaster. This is called flying at half-mast. At sea, lowering a ship's flag means surrender. As a result, most countries do not allow their flag to fly below another country's.

THE US FLAG AT THE WHITE HOUSE IS FLOWN AT HALF-MAST ON CERTAIN DAYS OF REMEMBRANCE.

BOY SCOUTS RETIRE
OLD US FLAGS DURING
A CEREMONY.

FLAG IT UP!

At the United Nations headquarters in New York City, over 190 national flags are displayed, each on its own flagpole and all at the same height. From Monday to Friday, the flags are raised every morning and lowered every evening, but only the larger United Nations flag flies on the weekends.

To Burn...

In the United States, damaged or worn flags cannot be thrown away. They have to be retired: Many thousands are burned in a ceremony by Boy Scouts, usually on the national flag day, June 14.

...Or Not to Burn

Many countries have laws that stop people burning or damaging their flags! For example, someone burning an Israeli flag could face a fine equal to $15,000. In Germany and China, a person can face up to three years in prison. Denmark is unusual. There, it is against the law to destroy the flag of any other nation, but not Denmark's own flag!

FLAG FAILS

When the Vice President met the leader of the European Union in Belgium in 2017, the US flag displayed behind the two politicians featured an embarrassing 51 stars, not 50 (*see right*). That's just one of many examples of flag flaws, fails, mistakes, and mix-ups.

COUNT THE NUMBER OF STARS...

FLAG IT UP!

The hot and sunny Turks and Caicos Islands are a British territory in the Caribbean Sea. The islands had a flaw in many of their flags from the 19th century until 1968. The flag was supposed to show piles of salt drying by the sea, but artists in Britain turned the salt into igloos made of ice and even drew a door in one of them (*see above*).

How Embarrassing

Sometimes, displaying the wrong flag can cause great embarrassment ... or even offense. In 1984, Canada was embarrassed when it flew hundreds of New Zealand flags to welcome the Australian prime minister.

Eight years later, it was Canada's turn to be outraged during the baseball World Series, when US soldiers displayed Canada's flag upside down by mistake. The US President had to make two public apologies to calm things down!

Rather Awkward

Organizers at the 2012 Olympics were red-faced when they displayed South Korea's flag at a North Korea vs. Colombia soccer match. South Korea is North Korea's bitter rival. The North Korean team walked off the field.

Crash!

Sometimes, it's not the flag's fault but the hardware it is attached to. In 1918, a group in Washington State started hoisting the world's largest flag (measuring 90 by 160 feet), but the fabric's 258-pound weight snapped the pole! When a second attempt was made a month later, the flag was torn away from the ropes that tied it to the pole!

CEREMONIES AND CELEBRATIONS

National flags are often flown on public holidays and to show support for the country's armed forces or athletes. Many nations also celebrate their country by having a flag day. In the United States, the date is June 14, the day in 1777 that the Stars and Stripes flag was adopted.

Flag Days

Flag days are often set on the date when a country, such as Afghanistan, Colombia, and Vietnam, became independent. In other countries, including Canada, Italy, and Bolivia, it is the day when the flag was first designed or flown.

Greenland, a territory of Denmark, got its own flag (*see below*) in 1985 and its own flag day in 2017, on June 21. The day is a public holiday.

FLAG IT UP!

In the Greek city of Athens, a flag ceremony is performed by soldiers called Evzones.

The Evzones raise and lower the flags at the ancient Acropolis every day in uniforms featuring a white kilt made of 100 feet of cloth with 400 pleats, representing the 400 years that Greece was occupied by the Ottoman Empire. The soldiers also wear *tsarouhia* shoes with a pom-pom on top.

GREENLAND'S FLAG DAY

Valdemar's Day

In Denmark, June 15 is celebrated as Valdemarsdag—the day the Danish flag is said to have fallen from the sky during a battle in 1219. (Not surprisingly, the battle ended in victory for the Danish king, Valdemar II.) Danish flags are flown throughout the country.

DESIGN YOUR OWN FLAG

Inspired by all the flags in this book? Why not try to make your own? All you need are some sheets of paper, pencils, and pens…and a lot of thought!

Flagging Up Questions

• What do you want your flag to show? National flags try to depict a whole country and its people in a single design. Can you sum yourself up with a flag design?

• Do you have one or more favorite colors?

• What symbol or shapes will you show on your flag? Will they represent where you live or a hobby or pet?

Sketch out different designs, aiming for something bold and simple so your flag can be seen from a distance. We've designed our own flag as an example (*see above left*)!

FLAG IT UP!

A NASA scientist has designed a flag for the planet Mars! Pascal Lee's tricolor features red for the red color of the planet, green for our exploration of it, and blue for the hope people will one day live on Mars!

Up the Pole

Copy your favorite design onto thick paper, leaving a 1.5-inch band empty at one side. Curl this band around a stick or plastic straw and stick it to the back of the paper using glue or staples.

Fabric Flag

If you have material and fabric markers or paints, you could make a cloth flag instead of a paper one. Mark out your design and color it in or use fabric glue to stick on shapes of cloth. You can staple or sew a pocket at one end of your flag to fit a pole.

OCEANIA

Oceania is the name for the region that holds Australia, New Zealand, New Guinea, and thousands of smaller islands scattered through the vast Pacific Ocean. There are 14 independent nations in Oceania, each with its own fascinating flag!

FIJI'S FLAG DISPLAYS BANANAS, SUGAR CANE, COCONUT PALMS, AND A DOVE!

AUSTRALIA

FIJI

Fiji's light blue flag symbolizes the Pacific Ocean.

KIRIBATI

MARSHALL ISLANDS

The star shows the islands' position just above the **Equator,** *which is represented by the diagonal stripe.*

MICRONESIA

The four stars stand for the nation's four states.

NAURU

On Nauru's flag, the star's 12 points represents the island nation's 12 tribes.

NEW ZEALAND

PALAU

PAPUA NEW GUINEA

SAMOA

SOLOMON ISLANDS

TUVALU

TONGA

VANUATU

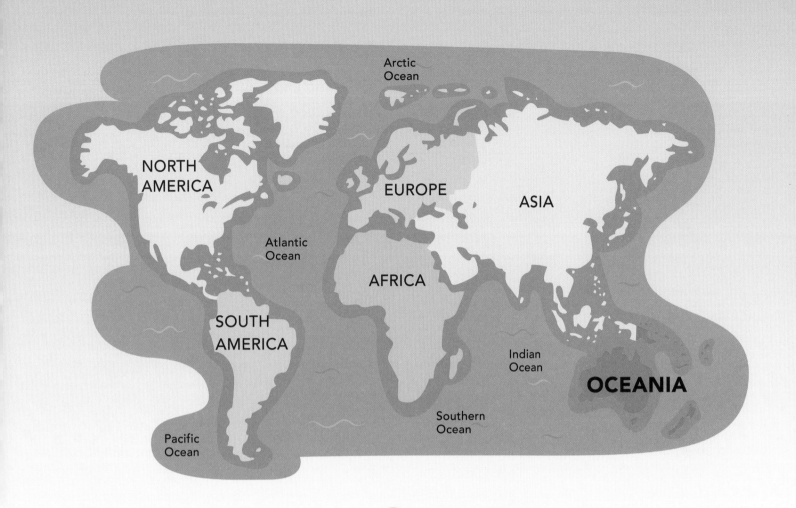

MANY OF THE NATIONS OF OCEANIA WERE ONCE BRITISH COLONIES. SOME OF THEM FEATURE A BRITISH UNION JACK (*SEE PAGE 43*) IN THE TOP LEFT OF THEIR DESIGN.

AUSTRALIA

NEW ZEALAND

TUVALU

FIJI

THE AUSTRALIAN FLAG

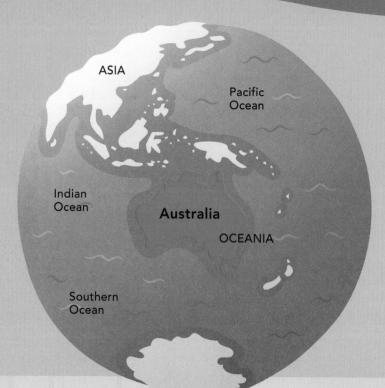

ASIA

Pacific Ocean

Indian Ocean

Australia

OCEANIA

Southern Ocean

In 1901, a competition was held to design a flag for the newly formed country of Australia. The prize was equal to four years' wages, so the competition attracted 32,823 entries.

Five winners with similar designs shared the prize. One of them was schoolboy Ivor William Evans.

THE FLAG OF AUSTRALIA

Starry Skies

The Australian flag features the five stars of the Southern Cross, the brightest constellation seen from the southern half of our planet. A constellation is a group of stars that seem to form a pattern in the night sky, though they may be millions of miles apart. (The Southern Cross is also featured on the flags of New Zealand, Papua New Guinea, and Samoa.)

A sixth, larger star, named the Commonwealth Star, has seven points. Six of the points represent the six states that came together to make up the new country of Australia. The seventh point was added in 1908 to represent Australia's overseas territories.

FLAG IT UP!

In 2015 and 2016, New Zealand held votes to decide whether to replace their flag (*see page* 86) with a new design featuring a white fern and no Union Jack. Some people felt that, as an independent nation, New Zealand's flag should no longer feature the Union Jack. Around 57 percent of the nation voted to keep their old flag.

FLUTTERING BIRDS

In 1971, 15-year-old Susan Karike was a student at Yule Island Mission School in New Guinea. Her teachers encouraged her to sketch out a flag. Little did Susan know that it would become the official flag of Papua New Guinea.

Bird of Paradise

Susan's Papua New Guinea flag has a background of black and red, which were popular colors in the region's folk art. Stars representing the Southern Cross (*see pages 88–89*) are in the black portion. The red half displays a Raggiana bird of paradise, which is native to New Guinea. The bird's feathers were used in ceremonial clothing for festivals.

FLAG IT UP!

In Vanuatu, boar tusks (*see above*) used to be prized as a symbol of wealth, and are still worn as jewelry. A boar's tusk is featured on the nation's flag (*see page* 86) along with *namale* fern leaves, which symbolize peace, and a yellow Y, which is the shape this group of islands forms in the ocean. The flag was adopted in 1980 when Vanuatu gained independence from France and Britain.

Frigate Bird

The flag of Kiribati is adorned with a frigate bird. The bird is known for its ability to fly long distances, which makes it ideal to represent Kiribati's 33 islands, which are scattered across 1.35 million square miles of the Pacific Ocean. On the flag, the bird flies above a sunrise, with blue and white wavy lines symbolizing the sea.

A FLAG QUIZ

So, you've read every page in the book. Do you think you are a flag expert? Test your memory and knowledge by taking this 30-question quiz. The answers are at bottom right. No peeking in advance!

1. Which nine nations have their flags pictured on pages 4–5?

2. Which country's national flag is known as the Stars and Stripes?

3. Claude Chappe invented a signaling system using two flags. Was it called wig-wag, flig-flag, or semaphore?

4. Which region of the United Kingdom is not represented on the Union Jack?

5. In which country did knights known as samurai sometimes display flags based on family badges?

6. Which pizza is said to have been created to match the colors of the Italian flag?

7. How many stripes are found on the Malaysian national flag?

8. Does Barbados, Jamaica, or Cuba's flag feature a three-pronged fork called a trident?

9. Which letter of the alphabet does this semaphore flag signal represent?

10. Which was the first country to fly its flag at the South Pole: Britain, Norway, Argentina, or Australia?

11. In 2007, which country planted its national flag at the bottom of the Arctic Ocean to mark the North Pole?

12. Which country is the only one to fly a five-sided national flag?

13. Which US state is the only one to feature a Union Jack on its state flag?

14. From 1880 to 1960, did the flag of French Sudan feature a spear, a stick man, or a tree in its design?

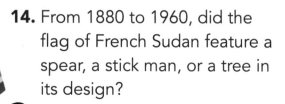

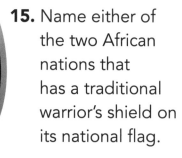

15. Name either of the two African nations that has a traditional warrior's shield on its national flag.

16. Which territory of Denmark flies the flag pictured directly above?

17. Was a vexillum a standard used by the armies of the ancient Aztecs, Chinese, or Romans?

18. Which region's flag features a bare-chested giant holding a club: Nunavut, Lapland, or Nebraska?

19. Which large Asian country has the same national flag design as Monaco?

20. In Gaelic football, what color flag is used to show a goal has been scored?

21. Which South American country had four different national flags all in the same year?

22. Did Bartholomew Roberts, Calico Jack Rackham, or Christopher Moody fly a pirate flag colored red?

23. What grade did Robert G. Heft originally get for designing the current United States national flag?

24. Which country had over 32,000 entries for the competition to design its flag?

25. Which country is the only one in the world with a national flag without any of the colors red, white, or blue on it?

26. At which Olympics did Haiti and Liechtenstein discover that their flag designs were the same?

27. Can you name three of the four flags flown at the peak of Mount Everest by Tenzing Norgay in 1953?

28. In which country would you find the national flag fluttering from the top of a 561-foot-high flagpole?

29. Which European nation's flag features a medal called the George Cross?

30. Who designed South Africa's flag in a week?

Answers

1. Jamaica, Sri Lanka, the USA, Panama, the Philippines, Georgia, Sweden, South Africa, Armenia
2. The United States
3. Semaphore
4. Wales
5. Japan
6. Margherita
7. 14
8. Barbados
9. K
10. Norway
11. Russia
12. Nepal
13. Hawaii
14. A stick man
15. Kenya or Swaziland
16. Greenland
17. The ancient Romans
18. Lapland
19. Indonesia
20. Green
21. Paraguay
22. Christopher Moody
23. B-
24. Australia
25. Jamaica
26. The 1936 Olympics
27. The United Nations, India, Nepal, and the UK
28. Saudi Arabia
29. Malta
30. Frederick Brownell

GLOSSARY

atmosphere
The blanket of gases that surrounds a planet or other body in space.

border
The line or boundary separating the territory of one country from another.

canton
The upper left quarter or of a flag, near the flagpole.

charge
A symbol or emblem found in the design of a flag.

coat of arms
A shield-shaped design representing a family, organization, or country.

colony
A region or country controlled and ruled by another country.

ensign
A flag flown on a boat or ship, or by a unit of a country's armed forces, to let others know what country it comes from.

equator
The imaginary line that runs around the center of the Earth, dividing it into halves or hemispheres.

European Union
Known as the EU for short, this is an organization to which many European countries belong. Countries in the EU share some of the same laws, and 19 of them use the Euro as money.

exile
Someone who has to live away from their own, home, country.

false colors
When a ship flies a flag to deceive others into thinking it is a different type of vessel.

fax machine
A machine that sent images and letters down a phone line to be printed by a fax machine at the other end.

guild
A group formed by people who shared similar work and banded together to protect their interests.

half-mast
When a flag is flown either halfway or below the top of the pole or staff. This is usually performed to commemorate the death of someone.

halyard
The rope used to raise or lower a flag.

headquarters
The main offices or base of an organization.

herald
A person, in the past, used to spot the flags, banners, and coats of arms of knights and other warriors and to record details and arrange processions.

heraldry
The study of coats of arms and the history of the families that they belong to.

hoist
The part of a flag nearest the flag staff or pole.

independence
When a country becomes free from the rule of another country and forms its own government.

Inuit
A number of native peoples from Greenland and far northern North America.

myth
A well-known story, often made up long in the past, which may not be true.

pioneered
When a person or group of people were the first to do something.

reign
The period when a king, queen, emperor, or some other ruler is in power in a country.

republic
A country that is governed by officials who have been elected by the people, and which has an elected president rather than a king or queen.

revolution
When a large group of people change the political system of their country, overturning those in power, often by using force.

samurai
High-ranking military figures and warriors in Japan in the past.

staff
The pole from which a flag is flown.

standard
A flag flown by an army or navy; or the personal flag of a king or queen.

submersible
An underwater vehicle used to dive deep below the sea's surface.

syllables
Parts of a word made up of single, unbroken sounds. "Cat" is one syllable.

symmetrical
When a design or object has two halves that are mirror images of each other.

territory
Land that is under the rule of another country.

tricolor
A flag whose design is made up of three blocks of colors. The flags of France and Italy are tricolors.

unfurled
To unroll or unwrap something such as a flag and spread it out.

United Nations
An organization to which all countries belong. Its aim is to promote peace and cooperation in order to solve some of the world's major problems.

vexillological
To do with the study of flags. People who study flags are vexillologists.

wig-wag
A signaling system invented in the 19th century, using one flag waved to the left and right of the signaler.

INDEX